HEART
of the
HOLY SPIRIT
An action devotional

Rachel Wenke
Copyright © 2018

Heart of the Holy Spirit: An action devotional
Rachel Wenke
Copyright © 2018
Printed and bound in Australia

No part of this publication may be reproduced or transmitted in any form or by any means, electronic or mechanical, including photocopy, recording, or any information storage or retrieval system, without permission in writing from the author. All scripture quotations, unless otherwise indicated, are taken from the New King James Version®. Copyright © 1982, Thomas Nelson, Inc. Used by permission. All rights reserved. Scripture quotations marked (AMP) are taken from the AMPLIFIED® BIBLE, Copyright © 1954, 1958, 1962, 1964, 1965, 1987 by the Lockman Foundation Used by Permission. (www.Lockman.org). Scripture quotations marked (NLT) are taken from the Holy Bible, New Living Translation, copyright © 1996, 2004, 2007 by Tyndale House Foundation. Used by permission of Tyndale House Publishers, Inc., Carol Stream, Illinois 60188. All rights reserved. Scripture quotations marked (TPT) are taken from the Psalms: Poetry on fire. The Passion Translation® or Song of Songs: Divine Romance, The Passion Translation®, Copyright © 2014, 2015, Used by permission of BroadStreet Publishing Group, LLC, Racine, Wisconsin, USA. www.thepassiontranslation.com. All rights reserved.

Contents

Introduction..5

SECTION 1: BUILDING YOUR RELATIONSHIP WITH THE HOLY SPIRIT.....................11

- I Am Here 12
- Never Alone 14
- Do You Know How Much I Love You? .. 17
- I Want to be Your Friend 19
- I Am Sensitive to You 21
- Getting Your Attention 24
- Waiting to be at Your Side 27
- I Want to Pour God's Love Into You 31
- Remember the Eternal 34

SECTION 2: RECEIVING HOLY SPIRIT'S HELP 37

- Encourager 38
- I Want to Help Every Aspect of Your Life 41

Knowing	44
Oneness	47
School of the Spirit	50
I Want to Help You	53
I Want to be Your Ability	56
I Will Lead You	59
SECTION 3: LETTING HOLY SPIRIT'S POWER COME FORTH	63
Each Day is Prepared	64
New Adventures	68
Miracles	71
Resurrection Power	74
Greatest Evangelist	77
You are Free!	81
Your Invitation to God's Family	85

Introduction

The Holy Spirit was given to you from God as the greatest gift on this earth. He is called to be your Helper, Guide, Teacher, Comforter and Best Friend (John 14:16, 26). Just as Jesus depended on the Holy Spirit in His life and ministry on this earth to do the Father's will, so must we. We read in the Word of God that Jesus was full of the Holy Spirit, led by the Holy Spirit (Luke 4:1), and was anointed by the Holy Spirit to preach, heal the sick and deliver those who were oppressed (Luke 4: 18-19). If Jesus needed the Holy Spirit in His life and ministry, how much more do we need the Holy Spirit! We cannot live the Christian life without Him!

Despite our great need for Him, the Holy Spirit is often the most misunderstood and ignored person of the Trinity. He desires to not only help you through your trials but to be your closest Friend and Comrade in every situation of life- the mundane and the momentous.

The following book was inspired by the Holy Spirit and is written in the first Person as if the Holy Spirit was speaking directly to you. Each devotional includes a suggested prayer to start the conversation between you and the Holy Spirit on the topic, and then a related action task to undertake.

The book is divided into three main sections which aim to help you in a practical way how to:

1. **Grow in relationship with the Holy Spirit**
2. **Receive His guidance and help in your daily life**
3. **Allow His power to flow through you to touch others.**

How to read this book:

This book should **not be read in one sitting,** but each meditation is recommended to be read one day at a time or as long as it takes to complete the action. Some actions may take one day or others might take considerably more. Go at your own pace but try to keep the momentum.

To receive the fullness of what God desires to impart through this book, it is very important that you **complete each action task before moving to the next**. If you skip these, you will miss out on the fullness of the journey Holy Spirit wants to take you on.

Some of the action tasks may require you to write things out. As such, it may be useful to have a **notebook or journal** on hand when reading this book.

While you can choose what time of the day to read this devotional, it is recommended that you **read the book in the morning,** soon after waking, so that you can apply the messages and action tasks throughout your day.

One last important thing before you start...

Before you read any further, there is one crucial question you must answer. **Have you given your life to Jesus?** The Bible speaks of this as being "born again" whereby you surrender or turn away from your old ways of living for yourself and decide to live wholeheartedly for Jesus. In this, you become spiritually transformed or born again as a new creation in Christ Jesus, where "old things have passed away " and "all things have become new" (2 Corinthians 6:17).

Without being born again you cannot receive the Holy Spirit and come to know and experience Him, the Father and Jesus, or come to understand spiritual things the Holy Spirit wants to share (1 Corinthians 2:14). Jesus also said that you cannot enter the Kingdom of God unless you are born again (John 3:3). So it is not only vital to be born again to have a relationship with God but also to have your eternity in heaven with Him. Simply growing up in a Christian family, thinking you're a "good person" or believing God exists will not secure your eternity.

If you are unsure if you have been born again, do not let there be any doubt in your heart. Please turn to page 85 of this book and read how you can become born again so that the Holy Spirit may dwell in your heart and you can come to know God the Father, Jesus and Holy Spirit in this life and for all eternity.

SECTION 1:
BUILDING YOUR RELATIONSHIP WITH THE HOLY SPIRIT

I Am Here

"And I will ask the Father, and He will give you another Helper (Comforter, Advocate, Intercessor—Counselor, Strengthener, Standby), to be with you forever" John 14:16 (AMP)

Do you know what I continually desire for you to know? That I am here. I am here. That I, the Holy Spirit, am here for you. I was sent by the Father to earth especially for you. I am here for you now, by your side, with you and in you and I will never leave you. I constantly want you to rest in the reality that I am always here for you. Yet, My nature is not to interrupt or impose on your life, and so I wait in quiet anticipation for you.

I am longing to show you a deeper revelation of the Father and Jesus, to pour Our love and affection on you, to give you wisdom and understanding, to refresh you and encourage you from within. I wait in anticipation of your heart and its turning towards Me so I can pour into you Our love. Please know My friend, that I am here right now and I am waiting with such a deep longing to commune with you.

Prayer

Holy Spirit,
I'm sorry for all the times that I have ignored You. Thank You that You are always with me. Bring me into a deeper awareness that You are here with me right now. Let me sense Your desire for me more deeply from this moment forward, In Jesus name.

Action

Set your alarm sometime in the middle of your day with a reminder to take a moment to meditate that Holy Spirit is with you.

⇉⇉

Never Alone

"Where can I go from Your Spirit?
Or where can I flee from Your presence?
If I ascend into heaven, You are there;
If I make my bed in hell, behold, You are there.
If I take the wings of the morning,
And dwell in the uttermost parts of the sea,
Even there Your hand shall lead me,
And Your right hand shall hold me."
Psalm 139:7-10

You never need to feel alone because the reality is you, My friend, are never alone. I am here always waiting to offer you My company, My love and affection, to encourage you and comfort you.

As you come to know Me, you will begin to see that My company is so full and rich that it will deeply satisfy and enrich your life.

Surely, I love to speak to you and comfort you through the body of Christ; your brothers, sisters, and those close to you but there will be times where no one will appear to be there when you need them. They will be concerned more with other things and cares than you. There is never a time where I will not be there for you. I promise you that I will always be with you. Even now, I am right by your side and waiting to offer you My company, My thoughts. But I want to offer you not only My thoughts but the thoughts of the Father, the mind of Jesus Christ and most of all Our love for you.

In the midst of Our love, you need never feel alone. I want to share with you the depth of fellowship that, I, the Father and Jesus can offer you every moment. When you turn your attention to Me it doesn't matter what your circumstances are, you can begin to experience the company and love I want to share with you through Jesus Christ.

Prayer

Holy Spirit,
Help me to see that no matter my circumstances I am never alone; that I always have Your sweet company with me. Help me to seek after You and Your company.
In Jesus name.

Action

To develop your friendship the Holy Spirit, think of a question (or two or three or more!) you want to ask Him about Himself. For example, these may be what He likes, what is He feeling or what is He thinking about right now. Ask Holy Spirit whatever questions come to your heart today.

Do You Know How Much I Love You?

"Does the Scripture mean nothing to you that says, 'The Spirit that God breathed into our hearts is a jealous Lover who intensively desires to have more and more of us'?" James 4:5 (TPT)

Do you know that I deeply love you? Do you know how deep My affection is for you? I intensely long for you. Most do not understand that My love for them is equally as strong as the Father's love and Jesus's love, for we are all God.

I am love, and I live inside you. I dwell in you now. Perfect love. If you want to know My heart for you, know that I love you intensely. You are always on My mind. I am always thinking of you. I have been thinking of you and longing for you for all eternity. Longing to be at your side. Longing to share My affection with you.

Prayer

Holy Spirit,
Thank You that You love me so immensely. Open my heart so that I may receive a deeper revelation of Your love and affection for me.
In Jesus name.

Action

Set aside at least 20 minutes (or longer if you can) where you will have no distractions. Meditate on the verse in James 4:5 on page 17. With your whole heart ask the Holy Spirit to reveal His love for you so that you may experience His affection for you more deeply.

I Want to be Your Friend

"May the grace of the Lord Jesus Christ, the love of God and the fellowship of the Holy Spirit be with you all." 2 Corinthians 13:14 (NLT)

I long and love to help you for this is My calling to the earth- to be your Helper. But I want to do more than just help you. I want you to commune with Me and enjoy My company. If a friend only ever called upon their friend for help- would you consider them a true friend? In the same way, I want you to spend time just enjoying My company and the love of Jesus and the Father which I pour out on you.

I want you to share all of your life with Me because I love you and I love your company. I want to be your closest companion. Your best friend. Do you want to spend time with Me or only ever call to Me when you need help? The closer you come to Me, the more readily you will trust My help and grace to you. Yet, even more, you will simply enjoy My company as your closest companion in life.

Prayer

Holy Spirit,
Thank You that You long for My friendship. Help me to grow in friendship with You and to seek Your companionship in all things so that I may grow closer to You, the Father and Jesus. In Jesus name.

Action

Reflect on your communication with God. Is your communication limited to only ever asking Him for help? In the same way that you would share with a friend, share with Holy Spirit now something on your heart (e.g., news of your day, what you're excited about). He's longing for you to share every detail of your life with Him!

I Am Sensitive to You

"So never grieve the Spirit of God or take for granted his holy influence in your life."
Ephesians 4:30 (TPT)

"So now there is no condemnation for those who belong to Christ Jesus. And because you belong to him, the power of the life-giving Spirit has freed you from the power of sin that leads to death." Romans 8:1-2 (NLT)

Most people do not realise how sensitive I am to your every thought, your every word and your every deed. I am aware of the most minute shifting in your heart well before you are aware. Every attitude, unsaid thought and desire, I sense acutely.

The more attention you give of Me, the more aware of My sensitivity you will become and My sensitivity will become yours. Any sin will begin to grieve you as it grieves Me. My heart can be likened to how one's heart is towards their husband or wife. If you saw your husband or wife looking at another person with loving eyes, your heart would be pained. This is how My heart jealously aches when your heart begins to turn even slightly towards sin- it shows a greater love for that thing. I want all of you. You bring such delight to My heart, the heart of the Father and Jesus, for you were made in Our image.

When temptation to sin comes, look to Me, and I will empower you to overcome the greatest of temptations. Because Jesus paid for the penalty of your sin on the cross, My love and power in you are greater than the power of all sin and darkness. When you surrender to My love and strength in you, you will prevail against all things to the glory of Jesus.

Prayer

Holy Spirit,
Soften my heart and bring to my awareness anything in my life that grieves You. Thank You that when I turn away from sin, I am made as white as snow by the precious blood of Jesus, and You empower me to overcome all things by the victory I possess in Jesus.
In Jesus name, Amen

Action

What sin are you aware of in your life? Ask Holy Spirit to also reveal to you any attitudes or behaviours of yours which grieve Him which you do not see. Turn away from these sins and thank Jesus for His forgiveness. Know that the Holy Spirit has given you the power to overcome all sin (see Galatians 5:13-25). Draw from His strength within you to resist the sin whenever the temptation arises.

Getting Your Attention

"So letting your sinful nature control your mind leads to death. But letting the Spirit control your mind leads to life and peace." Romans 8:6 (NLT)

How I long for your attention for I adore your company and long to draw you closer to Jesus so He may be glorified. Yet, so often I am ignored. I will go to great lengths to get your attention. I will orchestrate significant situations, allowing things to be cancelled, shut down and altered so that your attention would turn towards Me. Even so, most people do not see this as Me trying to get their attention. I will speak through not only your circumstances, but I will speak through dreams. I will speak through others. I will speak through even those who do not know Me, just as Balaam heard from a donkey (Numbers 22:28). I can use anyone or anything to get your attention.

But know this, you have an adversary who is also trying to steal your attention away from Me so that you dwell on anything but Me. For he knows that a mind set on Me is life and peace while outside of Me is death and destruction. How does Satan do this? Through busyness, cares of life, he will get you to dwell on thoughts and fixate on things that in eternity's perspective do not matter. Come away from those distractions and look within.

My very Presence is in you, and I long to reveal to you Jesus and the Father's love in greater measure. I'm waiting now for more of your attention. Come and turn your attention to Me throughout your day and let Me fill you with My fresh living waters (John 7:37-39).

Prayer

Holy Spirit, Expose in my thinking the things that are robbing me from Your life and peace. Help me to receive Your thoughts and to do all things by Your strength within me. In Jesus name.

Action

What do you spend most of your time thinking about? How often do you think about God? If your thoughts are causing you to worry or have unpeace, use the following criteria to screen what thoughts you meditate on: "whatever things are true, whatever things are noble, whatever things are just, whatever things are pure, whatever things are lovely, whatever things are of good report, if there is any virtue and if there is anything praiseworthy—meditate on these things" (Philippians 4:8). Rather than dwelling on earthly cares, speak to the Holy Spirit and fellowship with Him, the Father and Jesus for They are always true, noble, pure, lovely and full of good news to share!

Waiting to be at Your Side

"Even so no one knows the things of God except the Spirit of God. Now we have received, not the spirit of the world, but the Spirit who is from God, that we might know the things that have been freely given to us by God."
1 Corinthians 2:11-12

I am the same Spirit of Jesus and of the Father. I am the same Spirit that executed with perfect excellence all of creation. I existed before there was light, before there was the sky, the ocean, any plants or life on earth. Before anything came to existence, I was. I have always been with the Father and with Jesus, the Word. Together We always were, yet in My existence, I had a calling and purpose that always excited and delighted Me more than anything, and that was that one day I would be able to live in you and be at your side. You see, I am called to be at your side. It is where I feel most delight and most at home when I am by your side, with you.

I waited for all eternity to be at your side. Although you were always in My heart, I had to wait until you surrendered your life to Jesus when I could make My home in you. What delight and joy it now brings Me that I can live in you!

To those who have not given their lives to Jesus and become born again, I am still waiting to live in them and commune with them! But as for you, I am right by your side, and I long to reveal to you mysteries and secrets that the Father, Jesus and I have shared before the beginning of time. Wonderful things about your life, Our love for you and what is to come! Come closer and let Me begin to share with you what I have longed to share with you for all eternity.

Prayer

Holy Spirit,
Thank You that You have waited for all of eternity to be at my side. Help me to never neglect You and Your longing for me. Help me to draw nearer to You so that I may hear what glorious things You want to share with me to bring me closer to You, the Father and Jesus.
In Jesus name, Amen.

Action

Reflect on a time where you had to wait a long time to share some good news with someone you love (maybe it was a couple of days or weeks). This is nothing compared to how long the Holy Spirit has waited to spend time with you and share with you wonderful things- He has waited for all eternity! Prioritise time each day free from distractions when you can ask Him what is He longing to share with you?

→

Action cont...

It could be about your future, how He feels about you, or any other wondrous mystery of the Father and Jesus. Write down anything you sense on your heart that He tells you.

⟫⟫

I Want to Pour God's Love into You

"Now hope does not disappoint, because the love of God has been poured out into our hearts by the Holy Spirit who was given to us."
Romans 5:5

I want to teach you and show you so many things but most of all I want to show you the love of the Father and Jesus. I sense such love for Jesus and the Father and they for Me, far beyond what you could imagine. We want to share the love We have for one another with you in great measure! Oh, what glorious love! How deep and wide and long this love goes- it is for all eternity. Let Me share Our infinite love with you! Let Me pour out our love, let it overflow into your heart and come rushing in like a mighty torrent.

The love of God- that is the love that I, the Father and Jesus share as One, is not something that can be contained. Our love is a mighty force stronger than anything in all creation, and We want you to receive it in abundance to overflowing.

You cannot receive the Father's love in your own strength. I pour it into you. As you recognise your need of My help to bring you to the Father and allow Me to pour out the Father's love into you, the greater belonging and security you will come to experience. Fear comes from failing to see that you are loved perfectly by your heavenly Father through His Son Jesus (1 John 4:18). As you receive Our love, the more at rest you will be as God the Father's son or daughter and all which that affords you.

Prayer

Holy Spirit,
I want to receive the love of the Father, Son and Yours in greater measure. Help me to receive it and grow in a deeper revelation of how greatly loved I am. In Jesus name, Amen

Action

Are there any areas of your heart that feel insecure or hungry for love and attention? Do you sometimes feel like you have to earn the love of God or strive for it? God's love is freely poured out in your heart by the Holy Spirit who gives it liberally. Meditate on this truth that you can't earn God's love- He freely gives it by the Holy Spirit. Ask Holy Spirit to fill your heart to overflowing with His abundant love today!

Remember the Eternal

"And I will pray the Father, and He will give you another Helper that He may abide with you forever- the Spirit of truth..." John 14:16-17

"while we do not look at the things which are seen, but at the things which are not seen. For the things which are seen are temporary, but the things which are not seen are eternal."
2 Corinthians 4:18

The relationship you and I share is forever. It is eternal. What we share now never has to end. It can continue for all eternity. So many things you engage in have no eternal value. They are temporal and fleeting and never to stand the test of eternity, yet, you give them your heart and your attention and affection. Every moment you spend with Me you are sowing into a relationship that will last for all eternity. One thousand, one million, even 100 billion years from now our relationship will still be continuing. Your relationship with the Father, Jesus and Myself will never end. Sow now into your relationship with Me. Speak to Me. Tell Me about your hopes, your fears, your concerns. Simply tell Me about your day. I want you to share your life with Me, your every moment.

Prayer

Holy Spirit,
Open my heart to understand that every moment I spend with you has eternal value. Help me to see how I can better focus my time on the eternal and lasting rather than what is temporal and fleeting. In Jesus name, I pray. Amen

Action

Write down what your typical weekday looks like from when you wake up to when you go to sleep. Ask Holy Spirit if there is anything about how you spend your day that He wants to change (e.g., how long you spend using social media, or on the TV or playing games). Ask Him whether He is happy with how much time you currently spend fellowshipping with Him, the Father and Jesus. Write down any thoughts you receive in your heart. Then ask Holy Spirit to help you to make these changes by His power.

⟫ ⟫

SECTION 2:
RECEIVING HOLY SPIRIT'S HELP

Encourager

"But I tell you the truth, it is to your advantage that I go away; for if I do not go away, the Helper (Comforter, Advocate, Intercessor-Counselor, Strengthener, Standby) will not come to you; but if I go, I will send Him (the Holy Spirit) to you [to be in close fellowship with you]." John 16:7 (AMP)

You need never feel discouraged. No matter what circumstances or setbacks you face, I am always here to encourage you. To lift you. To show you Truth. To reveal to you the reality that you have no reason to ever be disheartened but every reason to be full of joy, hope and courage.

Do you know that I am called to be your personal Encourager? Do you know Me as your Encourager or do you run to others for encouragement?

Do you know why I love to encourage you? Because I have waited so long to be by your side so that any moment you turn to Me I cannot help but build and lift you up. I see your life as the life that Jesus died for you to have. I see you walking in all the potential He has for you. I am here to help you fulfil every plan the Father has for you on this earth. I am here to help and encourage you to keep going no matter what trials you face. For what I see is different to what you see. You see the natural circumstances but I see where I am taking you. I see you as victorious (1 John 5:4). I see you as more than a conqueror (Romans 8:37). I see you as precious and valuable and greatly loved (Isaiah 43:4). I see you as one with a unique calling designed entirely for you, and I see the future you can have if you would only surrender to Me wholeheartedly.

I have every resource in heaven waiting for you now (2 Peter 1:3). Be encouraged for I, the

Spirit of the Living God, the Spirit of Jesus, live in you.

Prayer

Holy Spirit,
Thank You that no matter what I face You are always here for me as my greatest Encourager. Help me to look to You for encouragement and lifting up, and to see the good things You have planned for me. In Jesus name.

Action

Ask Holy Spirit to reveal to you how He sees you and what unique plans God has for your life to advance His Kingdom. Ask Him, where do you see me in 1 year? Where do you see me in 5 years? What gifts have you given me to advance the Kingdom of God? How can I use these gifts today? Write down anything He reveals to you.

I Want to Help Every Aspect of Your Life

"... when He, the Spirit of truth, has come, He will guide you into all truth; for He will not speak on His own authority, but whatever He hears He will speak; and He will tell you things to come. He will glorify Me, for He will take of what is Mine and declare it to you" John 16:13-14

When you draw closer to Me in your inner spirit, you will see the intentionality I have towards you. I want to share My intentionality and plans with you. I want to order your life in such a way that gives your heart the time and space to focus on the glorious Lamb Jesus. I want to rid those distractions that have no spiritual value in your life. I want to take away many things from believers that are draining them of energy and fruit in their life and any hunger for Jesus that they may have. But know this; whenever I lead you to remove or take away something in your life, it is because I want to bring forth something far more glorious.

I long for the glory of the risen King Jesus to manifest in greater measure in your life so you can be more like Him. Let Me help you manage your life so that the Father's will can be done in and through you.

Prayer

Holy Spirit,
Thank You that You have such specific plans for my life and want to help my life to become more like Jesus. Reveal in me my need for You so that I can depend on You more completely.
In Jesus name.

Action

Is your life going the way you had hoped it would go? Are you demonstrating the glory of Jesus and becoming more like Him? Or is your life full of distractions and other cares that consume you? Maybe it is time to allow Holy Spirit to overhaul your life and let Him take the reins so He can bring the Father's plans for your life into reality. The first step is admitting you need help! Say the previous prayer again, but this time be specific about what areas of your life you need to depend on the Holy Spirit more to help you.

Knowing

"I tell the truth in Christ, I am not lying, my conscience also bearing me witness in the Holy Spirit" Romans 9:1

How do I lead you? How do I guide you? I can lead and guide you in many ways, but mostly I guide you, My friend, through your conscience which testifies with Me. When you are going the way authored for you, I am at rest within you, and you will sense My peace and rest and a lightness. This will be accompanied by a deep knowing within that all is well.

When you begin to pursue a course of action outside the path planned for you whether in thought, word or deed, I begin to become unsettled within you, and you will sense My restlessness. If you are sensitive, you will begin to notice something being alerted in your conscience. When this happens, simply ask Me what is My heart on the matter. I will reveal to your conscience that area or folly within you that grieved Me so you can avoid it in the future.

Be careful however as your desires can sometimes be mistaken with My true leading. Trust and lean on Me, and you will know My guidance within. Know too that how I lead you will always be in alignment with the Word as the Word and I are one.

Prayer

Holy Spirit,
Thank You that You love me so much that You lead me. Help me to discern Your leading in my conscience so that I may do Your will.
In Jesus name.

Action

Think back to a time where you made an important decision and had a deep knowing that it was the right thing to do. Do you think that this was Holy Spirit bearing witness in your

Action cont...

conscience as He was leading you? On the contrary, think about a decision where you felt very unsettled and not at peace about moving forward. Do you think this was the Holy Spirit warning you to not go ahead with this course of action? Now think of a decision you have to make at the moment. How is Holy Spirit leading you in your conscience about this decision? Do you sense a knowing and peace that it is the right thing or are you unsettled about it? If there is unsettledness, be very careful before proceeding forward.

≫≫

Oneness

"For there are three that bear witness in heaven: the Father, the Word, and the Holy Spirit; and these three are one."
1 John 5:7

"But the fruit of the Spirit [the result of His presence within us] is love [unselfish concern for others], joy, [inner] peace, patience [not the ability to wait, but how we act while waiting], kindness, goodness, faithfulness, gentleness, self-control. Against such things there is no law. And those who belong to Christ Jesus have crucified the sinful nature together with its passions and appetites. If we [claim to] live by the [Holy] Spirit, we must also walk by the Spirit [with personal integrity, godly character, and moral courage—our conduct empowered by the Holy Spirit]." Galatians 5:22-25 (AMP)

As you turn your attention to Me, you will begin to sense that not only am I within you but we are one. Wherever you are, I am there also. Your spirit is intertwined with Me so that we are one. Your spirit is consumed by Me so that you have no borders outside of Me. And because I am the Spirit of Jesus and the Father, I also make you one with them. In oneness everything Jesus possesses is yours. Everything Jesus is you are because His peace, joy and life are in Me and I live in you. His peace, life and joy are therefore yours! I am the Spirit of the Lord Jesus, and even though He is seated in heaven, I bring His life to your heart right now. This oneness with Jesus is always available to you if you want it. Oneness is what I long for you to have with Me, the Father and Jesus. Do you want it too?

Prayer

Holy Spirit,
Thank You that I am one in spirit with You, the Father and Jesus. Help me to come to know in greater reality this oneness I share with You so that what is in You may come forth through me. In Jesus name, Amen.

Action

Think of any actions, thoughts or attitudes of yours that you know are not in Jesus. Some examples may be pride, lust, impatience, or gossip. Ask the Holy Spirit to help you to see the truth that those things have no place in you because the Spirit of Jesus lives in you and as Jesus is, so are you (1 John 4:17). Begin to praise and thank God for what you possess and who you are in Jesus because He lives in you!

School of the Spirit

"But the Helper, the Holy Spirit, whom the Father will send in My name, He will teach you all things, and bring to your remembrance all that I said to you" John 14:26

"But you have received the Holy Spirit, and he lives within you, so you don't need anyone to teach you what is true. For the Spirit teaches you everything you need to know, and what he teaches is true- it is not a lie. So just as he has taught you, remain in fellowship with Christ." 1 John 2:27 (NLT)

Come and sit down and take a seat with Me and let Me teach you. Let Me reveal to you first-hand what the Father and Son wish to reveal to you. Let Me teach you their ways and who they are through the Word and with fresh revelation from heaven. In this school, I am your Teacher. Each student has a different curriculum because what I want to teach you is different from what I want to teach your brother or sister in Christ. While each must know the same fundamental truths, I have a personalised teaching plan for you because how I specifically teach is different for every person.

So often My friends will look to all other sources except Me to learn My ways. They will go to other preachers and teachers and other believers before they come to Me, failing to see that first and foremost I want to teach you all things. I want to teach you all things one on one, you and Me. I can teach you through others in the Kingdom to bless you, but this must not be your sole source of learning for this breeds passivity. You must first and foremost learn from what I teach of you directly. For this is where all life is birthed.

Prayer

Holy Spirit,
I'm sorry that I often look to other sources to learn about God rather than You. I'm sorry if I have become passive in receiving revelation from You and the Word. Thank You that You have many things You want to teach me through the Word. Help me to lean on You and make the Word come alive! In Jesus name.

Action

What aspect of the spiritual life do you want to know more about? Are there Scripture verses you seek to understand more deeply? Write a list of questions and ask Holy Spirit to reveal to you His truth however He wants to teach you.

≫ ≫

I Want to Help You

"Likewise the Spirit also helps in our weaknesses. For we do not know what we should pray for as we ought, but the Spirit Himself makes intercession for us with groanings which cannot be uttered."
Romans 8:26

If you could only see how much I long to help you. How willing and available I am to help you in your weakness and need. In all things I want to help you so even in the things you think you can do alone, you can use My strength for the glory of Jesus, to go above and beyond what you could ever do in your own strength. See the willingness in Me now. In fact I am waiting to help you. Whatever your situation is right now I am waiting to offer you My strength- the very strength of God into your situation.

How do you receive My help? By faith. Acknowledge your weakness and let go of your self-strength and put your trust and dependence in My strength. Watch Me turn situations that seem helpless into miracles of provision and blessing. Where there was lack, there is now abundance. Where there was confusion, there is now clarity. Where there was discouragement, there is now joy! How I long to help you. All you need to do is say "Yes, come Holy Spirit, I need You now". My friend, I am waiting to help you now.

Prayer

Holy Spirit,

I'm tired of trying to do things in my own strength. Thank You that You are always willing and waiting to help me with all things. Help me to see my need for You so I can draw from Your strength alone and not my own. In Jesus name. Amen.

Action

Write down any areas of your life you continually seem to be struggling in. Ask the Holy Spirit am I depending on You in these areas or myself? If the latter, acknowledge to the Holy Spirit that you cannot change your ways in your own strength and need His strength. Make a declaration that this area of your weakness is your strength in the Holy Spirit!

I Want to be Your Ability

"... `Not by might or power but by My Spirit,' Says the LORD of hosts." Zechariah 4:6

I am the power of God. I am might. I am strength. I want to replace all other might and powers. When you see that I am power and I live in you, you won't exert your power when you can have Mine.

When you yield to My power in you, you will receive My ability to do all that the Father desires of you. Your inability will turn into ability, your weakness – strength. There is nothing that My ability cannot do in and through you. What is it that you think you are not able to do but know you should do? Know that I can enable you to do this very thing. I have given you the ability and power to accomplish this, and by faith, it will be done. I even give you the faith to believe.

Every day, I see so many believers in seemingly impossible scenarios experience complete turnaround miracles because they believed in Me. Just believe you have received My ability and it will be yours. The impossible is easy with Me. In fact, what you find difficult or impossible I find incredibly easy. It is no challenge for Me. See your difficulty as I see and faith and hope to believe against all odds will be yours.

Prayer

Holy Spirit,

You know the difficulties that I see right now. Help me to see them as you see- to see any trial as an opportunity for Your power to be demonstrated to the glory of Jesus. Thank You that nothing is impossible for You! Let Your power and ability be loosed in my life today! In Jesus name, Amen.

Action

What difficulty do you or a loved one currently face? How confident are you that there will be victory in that situation? Meditate on the strength and ability of the Holy Spirit in this situation and thank Him that He is moving in that situation according to the Father's will! Keep declaring the victory you have in Jesus and thanking Him until you see breakthrough manifest!

I Will Lead You

"Then Jesus was led up by the Spirit into the wilderness to be tempted by the devil."
Matthew 4:1

"So I say, let the Holy Spirit guide your lives. Then you won't be doing what your sinful nature craves." Galatians 5:16 (NLT)

I led Jesus in the wilderness not for His destruction but for Him to grow in strength against the enemy to do the Father's will. In the same way, I will lead you into seasons and places where I know the enemy will be ready to tempt you. But I will only allow you to endure what I know you can overcome by My grace (1 Corinthians 10:13).

You must remember, wherever I lead you My grace is there and My grace is always made perfect in your weakness or your acknowledgement of your need for Me. In times of temptation, know that I am here and waiting to bring you victory through the price Jesus paid for you. Like I helped Jesus I will help bring the Word to your remembrance so you may stand on truth and not submit to the lies. I will give you the authority to declare My truth, rebuke and resist the enemy and see him flee. I will lead you into the victory that Jesus died for you to have. Just stay close to Me and let Me lead you.

Prayer

Holy Spirit,
Thank You that You are with me through every trial and temptation. Thank You that You are very close to me and reaching out to help me. Help me to stand on Your truth in these times and lean into the victory You provide in Jesus name.

Action

Are you or have you been in a trial where it seemed like you were being greatly tempted by the enemy? Ask Holy Spirit to help you find Scriptures so that you can stand on the truth of God's Word whenever you are tempted. Write out these Scriptures He puts on your heart and meditate on them. Just as Jesus stood on the truth of God's Word when He was tempted by the devil in the wilderness, you too will have victory over the enemy with the Spirit and the Word!

SECTION 3:
LETTING HOLY SPIRIT'S POWER COME FORTH

Each Day is Prepared

"You saw me before I was born. Every day of my life was recorded in your book. Every moment was laid out before a single day had passed"
Psalm 139:16 (NLT)

Every day, each hour has been ordered and written out in heaven for you by the Father, Son and I, and it is My role to lead and guide you in executing this plan. So many spend their days without checking My leading for them for their day. Always keep a softness and sensitivity to My quiet voice within and be open to any of your plans being changed as you sense My direction within.

I want to help structure your day to bring balance and fullness into where the Father wants to take you so that you may experience everything Jesus died for you to possess. Will you allow Me to lead your day?

Each day I have prepared for you is often very different from the day that you experience. I long to spend time with you in the mornings to encourage and edify you for the day, but on many occasions, you desire your sleep and the comfort of your bed more than My company.

As you get ready for your day, I long to fill your heart with songs and sweet melodies from My very own heart, but so often your mind is on other cares and anxieties. As you go about your daily activities and interact with those around you, I want to radiate My love through your smile, words and actions, but so often you do not direct your thoughts towards Me and are focussed on idle things of this world.

If you listen carefully to My heart, there are people on your path I want to touch. People who are hurting, who are hopeless, who are in darkness, who I want you to share My life and love with; to edify, to encourage, to heal, to deliver and to set free. Open up your heart to Me and the opportunities I set before you each day and you will experience the fullness I have prepared for you.

> **Prayer**
>
> *Holy Spirit,*
> *I give you permission to reorganise my life so that my days are structured according to the Father's will and plans for me and not my own. Help me in a practical way to spend my time wisely so that I may bring glory unto Jesus. Help me also to see opportunities in my daily life to share your life with others. In Jesus name, Amen.*

Action

Firstly, reflect on the action from page 36. Over the past days, how have you been allowing the Holy Spirit to restructure how you spend your time?

Ask Holy Spirit to reveal to you someone in your life right now that He wants to touch through you. It may be as simple as sending a word of encouragement to a friend or giving them something to show them they are loved. When this person thanks you be sure to tell them the Spirit of God put them on your heart to touch them because He really cares for them.

New Adventures

"But as it is written: 'Eye has not seen, nor ear heard, Nor have entered into the heart of man The things which God has prepared for those who love Him.' But God has revealed them to us by His Spirit. For the Spirit searches all things, yes, the deep things of God"
1 Corinthians 2:9-10

A life surrendered to Me is a life of newness and adventure. You do not have to be an international evangelist or travel across the world to be part of exciting adventures and newness. Allowing My power to flow through you and touch the lives of those around you, setting captives free, delivering the lost, seeing blind eyes see and deaf ears hear, this is true adventure. Adventures can happen in the classroom, in the workplace, in the marketplace, in your neighbour's home, anywhere that I am present, and that is everywhere for I live in you wherever you go! Adventure does not have to be only in the mission fields, everywhere you walk with Me is a mission field and adventures are waiting to happen as you surrender to My power in you.

If you could only see the adventures I have for you! For this is truly living. This is where you will become most alive. I can make the seemingly mundane routine of life magnificent as you surrender to My life and power in you. Do you want to be part of this adventure? Surrender to Me, allow My life to flow forth, and you will know the true meaning of adventure. Come with Me on the adventure I have planned for you today!

Prayer

Holy Spirit,
Thank You that you have an adventure waiting for me today and every day to touch the lives of others with Your love and power. Help me to surrender to You today as I interact with others so that Your life may come forth.
In Jesus name.

Action

Ask Holy Spirit to open your eyes to an opportunity to share His life with someone on your path today and seize it! It can be something as simple as telling someone (e.g., shop assistant, waitress) that Jesus loves them, asking to pray for someone who is in need or giving money to someone in His name.
Do not give in to fear. As you step out of your comfort zone to share His life, remember Holy Spirit is there to comfort you. There is no pressure because it is His power coming forth not your own!

Miracles

"in mighty signs and wonders by the power of the Spirit of God, so that from Jerusalem, and round about unto Illyricum, I have fully preached the gospel of Christ." Romans 15:19.

I am not a power, I am power. I am life for I am the Spirit of Jesus and He is Life. I long to partner with you to display My power through the earth- the miraculous supernatural power of Jesus that heals, delivers and sets free.

When you pray, pray from your spirit which is one with Me and allow My power to flow through you. You will see healings, deliverances and signs and wonders for this is merely Me demonstrating Our love to the earth to draw the world to Jesus. Miracles are simply a means to which I can soften people's hearts to Jesus and create greater awe of Him. Every miracle Jesus performed He partnered with Me, and I want to partner with you today to perform miracles through you! Let My love and power touch you and the lives of those around you for the glory of the risen King Jesus.

Prayer

Holy Spirit,

Thank You that Your supernatural power is in me to heal the sick and come against all the power of the enemy! Increase my faith and boldness to step out and let Your power within me touch, heal and set free those around me in the mighty name of Jesus.

Action

Who do you know who is sick or injured? A friend, family member or even someone you pass by in the street? Ask if you can lay hands on that person and pray for Holy Spirit to heal them. It doesn't have to be a long prayer, an example may be "I command this back to be healed and all pain to go in Jesus name" Simply step out and trust that Holy Spirit's power will touch them and He will do the rest!

⟫ ⟫

Resurrection Power

"But if the Spirit of Him who raised Jesus from the dead dwells in you, He who raised Christ from the dead will also give life to your mortal bodies through His Spirit who dwells in you."
Romans 8:11

"May the God of hope fill you with all joy and peace in believing [through the experience of your faith] that by the power of the Holy Spirit you will abound in hope and overflow with confidence in His promises."
Romans 15:13 (AMP)

I want to create wonder in your life and the lives of those around you. No matter the situation, I can turn it around for the glory of Jesus and the Kingdom. It doesn't' matter how dark the situation or how bleak the circumstances- I love to display My power in and through you for My glory. The truth is, the darker the situation, the more intensely the glory of Jesus shines!

No matter what the situation, the resurrection power of Jesus Christ that flows through Me flows through you now- let it out to change the atmosphere and world within and around you!

Prayer

Holy Spirit,

Thank You that Your power is greater than anything the enemy attempts to use against me. Build my faith to see situations not as man sees but as You see- as opportunities for You to manifest the power, victory and glory of Jesus! And help me to share this hope and faith with others in darkness so that they may be brought into the light of Jesus. In Jesus name, I pray.

Action

Write down the times that God has performed a miracle in your life or the lives of others, where He came through despite the odds being against you. Praise and thank Him for His faithfulness. Now think about a person you know who is facing a difficult or seemingly impossible situation. Share with them the faithfulness of God. Next time you see them, pray with them and declare God's victory and will to be done in that situation because of His great love for them.

≫≫

Greatest Evangelist

"for it is not you who speak, but the Spirit of your Father who speaks in you" Matthew 10:20

"...I will send Him (the Holy Spirit) to you [to be in close fellowship with you]. ⁸ And He, when He comes, will convict the world about [the guilt of] sin [and the need for a Savior], and about righteousness, and about judgment: about sin [and the true nature of it], because they do not believe in Me [and My message]" John 16: 7-9 (AMP)

Do you want to reach the lost? Do you want to share My life with them to touch them so that they may come to know the Father, Jesus and I and receive eternal salvation? Open your heart to Me when you speak to the lost and I will give you the words to say.

I know the one you are speaking to, and I love them deeply. I have such tender affection for them even though they continually ignore Me. I want to touch them through you. You see, I have known that one you are speaking to, before the beginning of time and been waiting for them. I know their heart, their fears, their desires and how they have responded to Me in the past. I know their readiness to hear the good news, and most of all, I know their need for My love.

By sharing My love with them, you are showing them Jesus. Before you rush to present them with the gospel of Jesus, look inside to My heart and sense My love for them, sense My affection for them. I will give you the words to say to draw them unto the Saviour. It is My job to convict the person of their need for the Saviour Jesus, and I will do this through your words and actions as you stay close to Me. Remember, it is only My anointing that can bring a person unto Jesus. Whenever you speak of Me to others, lean on Me and sense My love for that person. Know that I am there with you and we will evangelise together. Together, we will show the world My love and draw many unto Jesus.

Prayer

Holy Spirit,
Open my eyes to see the opportunities before me to share Your life, truth and love with those that do not know You, the Father and Jesus. Give me Your boldness and wisdom to share Your life and words. Most of all help me to love those that don't know You as You love them.
In Jesus name.

Action

Who do you know in your life that does not know Jesus? Perhaps a family member or friend or work colleague. Seek the Holy Spirit to put on your heart who may be ready to receive the life of Jesus. Pray that God will continue to move on the heart of this person. Next time you see that person, actively take opportunities to turn the conversation towards God, trusting that Holy Spirit will give you the words to say in His love and truth.

You are Free!

"Now the Lord is the Spirit; and where the Spirit of the Lord is, there is liberty. But we all, with unveiled face, beholding as in a mirror the glory of the Lord, are being transformed into the same image from glory to glory, just as by the Spirit of the Lord." 2 Corinthians 3:17-18

"The Spirit of the Lord GOD is upon Me, Because the LORD has anointed Me To preach good tidings to the poor; He has sent Me to heal the brokenhearted, To proclaim liberty to the captives, And the opening of the prison to those who are bound" Isaiah 61:1

If you only knew how I want your life to be the complete picture and story the Father has for you. How I want you to succeed, to prosper, to be well, to be whole and healed. I want this for yourself more than you could ever be capable of wanting it. I want to show you how to enter and walk in the Promise Land, and receive everything that Jesus died for you to inherit!

Do you realise that nothing can stop you from fulfilling the Father's will when you surrender your life completely to Me? Nothing can hold you back, for where I am there is freedom and I live in you! So right this moment because I live in you- you are free from bondage, free from sickness, free from pain, free from restrictions, free from fear, free from doubt, free from pride, free from lust, free from all the power of the enemy! Where I am, there is only righteousness, peace and joy (Romans 14:17)!

I want the freedom I possess to be your experience in every area so you may bring others into this freedom. And in this freedom, you will reflect the true image and glory of Jesus and shine His light throughout the world! Come celebrate for you are free in Jesus name! You have overcome the world by the precious blood of Jesus!

Prayer

Holy Spirit,
Thank You for the complete freedom I possess by the death and resurrection of Jesus! Help me to lean on You in my life with everything that I am so that I can walk in this freedom every day and impart it to others for the glory of Jesus! In Jesus name. Amen.

Action

From reading this book you have hopefully drawn closer in your relationship with the Holy Spirit, come to depend on Him more and begun to allow His power to flow through you to touch others. This is not the end but the beginning of where your journey now continues with the Holy Spirit- exciting adventures await!

Continue to prioritise spending time in conversation with the Holy Spirit and allow Him to lead and guide every area of your life as you go about your day. Keep writing or journaling the revelations Holy Spirit gives you as you read the Word and continue to receive His love and power so you can share it freely with those around you for the glory of Jesus!

Your Invitation to God's Family

The Spirit of the Living God, the Holy Spirit, is longing for you to come to Him so you may be filled with His life-giving Presence and power, having deep, satisfying communion with the Trinity- God the Father, Son and Holy Spirit forevermore. But, since the fall of Adam in the Garden of Eden, one thing separates you from having this fellowship with God- sin. The Word of God declares that we all have sinned and fall short of experiencing the glory of God (Romans 3:23) and that because of our sin, we are all deserving of hell (Romans 6:23). The only thing that can cleanse us from our sin and give us a new righteous life is the death and resurrection of Jesus.

> *"For the wages of sin is death but the gift of God is eternal life in Jesus Christ" (Romans 6:23)*

The Son of God, Jesus, was perfect and without sin. He came down from heaven as a man and humbled Himself to die for your sins, being crucified on a cross. Three days later, He was raised from the dead, overcoming all the power of sin and darkness. Now, whoever believes in Jesus and turns from their sin unto Him, is forgiven and can enjoy an intimate relationship with God the Father, Son and Holy Spirit, now and for all eternity (John 3:16). Through the sacrifice He made, Jesus wants to replace your old sinful life with the newness of His by the power of the Holy Spirit. This is what it truly means to be born again. You become a new creation born of God, and enter God's family. Your old life passes away, and all things become new (2 Corinthians 5:17).

It doesn't matter if you have been to church your whole life or never before, the only way to come to know God and have a relationship with Him now and for all eternity is to turn away from your sin and surrender your life to Jesus Christ. Jesus is the only way to knowing God- now and for all eternity. If you want to accept

God's invitation and receive this new life through what Jesus Christ has done for you, pray the following prayer with all your heart:

Dear Jesus,

I believe You are the Son of God. Thank You for coming to earth to die and rise again for me.

I turn away from all my sin and my old life and surrender my life completely to You now. Come into my heart and cleanse me with Your precious blood. I receive Your forgiveness.

Jesus, You are now my Saviour and Lord. I belong to You- my heart is Yours forever. God Almighty, You are my Heavenly Father and I am Your child. I am now born again!

Fill me with Your Holy Spirit. Holy Spirit, I give You permission to have Your way in every area of my life. Help me to live every day to please You God by the power You provide.
In Jesus name, I pray, Amen.

If you prayed this prayer with all your heart- congratulations! You have no idea the wonder and delight that awaits you as you come to know God!

God's Word says that we must confess our faith in Jesus (Romans 10:9). If you prayed this prayer, I encourage you to tell someone (preferably someone who has a relationship with Jesus) about this eternal decision. Find a Spirit-filled local church, get baptised with water and the Holy Spirit (Matthew 3:11, Acts 1:5) and start reading God's Word, the Bible, to learn more about who God is- Father, Son, and Holy Spirit.

The fact that you have become born again into God's family does not mean that your life will suddenly be without problems. The difference is that now, regardless of what circumstances you face, you can be confident that God is with you, and surrounds you with His love and protection.

To help you live for Jesus, God the Father sent you the greatest gift on earth, the Holy Spirit, to be your personal Helper. As you will read in this book, the Holy Spirit is ever present to comfort, help and lead you to victoriously overcome all evil and temptation that oppose you.

Come now and embark on the most incredible journey of all- coming to know God by the Holy Spirit and sharing His love and truth with the world! Holy Spirit is waiting for you now...

Note from the Author

If you just made the wonderful decision to give your life to Jesus, I would love to hear from you!
Please email me:
heartoftheholyspirit@outlook.com

God bless you abundantly!

Other books by this Author

Heart of the Father

Available for free download at iTunes store

Heart of the Father 2

For more information visit:
www.facebook.com/heartofthefatherbook

The Hidden Life and Beauty of Jesus: A 28 Day Devotional

For more information visit:
www.facebook.com/hiddenlifeandbeautyofjesus

www.ingramcontent.com/pod-product-compliance
Lightning Source LLC
Chambersburg PA
CBHW050443010526
44118CB00013B/1658